MW00395444

there is more to your story

a study of hope from the book Ruth

BOBI ANN ALLEN

Copyright © **2018 by Bobi Ann Allen**

All rights reserved.

Published in the United States of America.

ISBN-13:
978-1984224644
ISBN-10:
1984224646

No part of this book may be reproduced in any form unless written permission is granted from the author or publisher. No electronic reproductions, information storage, or retrieval systems may be used or applied to any part of this book without written permission.

Due to the variable conditions, materials, and individual skills, the publisher, author, editor, translator, transcriber, and/or designer disclaim any liability for loss or injury resulting from the use or interpretation of any information presented in this publication. No liability is assumed for damages resulting from the use of the information contained herein.

All scripture quotations, unless otherwise indicated, are taken from the Holy Bible, New International Version®, NIV®. Copyright © 1973, 1978, 1984, 2011 by Biblica, Inc.™ Used by permission of Zondervan. All rights reserved worldwide. www.zondervan.com. The "NIV" and "New International Version" are trademarks registered in the United States Patent and Trademark Office by Biblica, Inc.™

DEDICATION

To the women who have modeled what it is to persevere with hope. I have admired and been inspired to press on because of you.

How To Use This Book

This book was written to correspond with the free There Is More To Your Story teaching found at thereismore.net. Each week begins with a video lesson and is followed by five days of homework.

This study is appropriate for any spiritual maturity level and can be done individually or with a small group.

Small Groups:

When using within a small group, encourage the group to highlight or underline parts of the homework that impacted or spoke to them. At the start of your time together, take time to review the highlighted homework from the previous week and share what you learned.

Following each video, allow time for group members to answer the reflection questions and then discuss their answers along with the provided discussion questions below the videos.

CONTENTS

ACKNOWLEDGMENTS

First, thank you to Jesus, who took the little I had and decided it was enough to use. You took my ugly and turned it into something I didn't recognize. I still stand amazed that I get to be part of your kingdom work. Thank you to my best friend and the love of my life, Jared, for tirelessly believing in me and earnestly working to help me fulfill the purpose for which God created me. Thank you to my Kati Ann and Kie for showing me a new part of me and joining the adventure of living for Jesus. And finally, to my parents, who have instilled within me the confidence to just go for it.

1

the back story

notes:

"In the days when the judges ruled, there was a famine in the land. So a man from Bethlehem in Judah, together with his wife and two sons, went to live for a while in the country of Moab."—Ruth 1:1

Time period Ruth was written in: period of the Judges

We could sum up the lesson we learn from the Judges cycle in one sentence: God is faithful even when we are not.

Obedience in the context of Christian community is of absolute importance in our lives.

notes:

And when all these things come upon you, the blessing and the curse, which I have set before you, and you call them to mind among all the nations where the Lord your God has driven you, and **return to the Lord your God**, you and your children, and obey his voice in all that I command you today, with all your heart and with all your soul, then the Lord your **God will restore** your fortunes and have mercy on you, and **he will gather you again** from all the peoples where the Lord your God has scattered you. If your outcasts are in the uttermost parts of heaven, from there the Lord your God will gather you, and from there he will take you. And the Lord your God will bring you into the land that your fathers possessed, that you may possess it. And he will make you more prosperous and numerous than your fathers. (emphasis added)

—Deuteronomy 30:1-5

The word is very near you. It is in your mouth and in your heart, so that you can do it. "See, I have set before you today life and good, death and evil. If you obey the commandments of the Lord your God that I command you today, by loving the Lord your God, by walking in his ways, and by keeping his commandments and his statutes and his rules, then you shall live and multiply, and the Lord your God will bless you in the land that you are entering to take possession of it. But if your heart turns away, and you will not hear, but are drawn away to worship other gods and serve them, I declare to you today, that you shall surely perish.

Therefore choose life, that you and your offspring may live.

—Deuteronomy 30:14-19
(emphasis added)

If you think you've
blown God's plan
for your life, rest in
this. You, my
beautiful friend, are
not that powerful.
-Lisa Bevere

Reflection

When have you found yourself in the middle of someone's (yours or someone else's) tragic mistake? What were the consequences that came as a result of that mistake?

What comfort do you find knowing that men and women have been making a mess of their lives for centuries? How might your life look different if God hadn't redeemed their mess?

Week 1 Day 1

When The Judges Rule

Read Ruth 1:1-5

Key Verse:

> *"In the days when the judges ruled, there was a famine in the land. So a man from Bethlehem in Judah, together with his wife and two sons, went to live for a while in the country of Moab."*
> — Ruth 1:1

During what time in Israel's history does this story take place?

_____

The book preceding Ruth ends with these words, "In those days there was no king in Israel: every man did that which was right in his own eyes." (Judges 21:25 KJV)

What do we learn about the spiritual state of Israel during this time?

_____

_____

_____

Given Israel's spiritual condition at the time, what might explain the famine? (Deut. 28:15, 22-24)

_____

The name "Bethlehem" means "house of bread." Why is that name ironic based on the situation facing the family in our story?

During the time of the judges, the Israelites demonstrate a cycle of sin and salvation that becomes a pattern for God's people.

According to the diagram, which step in the cycle were the Israelites experiencing at the start of our story?

As Christians, sometimes we feel we are stuck in a pattern of *sin and salvation* types of experiences with God. We keep falling into the same patterns of sin. Our walk with Christ doesn't feel like progress but more like going two steps forward and then two steps back. It's like being on a spiritual roller coaster with God, with ups and downs that make us wonder what lies ahead.

What are some areas in your life (family, work, church, school, etc.) where you've tried to bring about change, only to be disappointed in your lack of progress?

_____

_____

_____

Spend some time talking to God about your frustrations. Express to Him your heart's desire for your spiritual life.

_____

_____

_____

_____

_____

_____

_____

_____

_____

_____

_____

_____

_____

_____

Moab

Read Ruth 1:1-5

Key Verse:

> *"In the days when the judges ruled, there was a famine in the land. So a man from Bethlehem in Judah, together with his wife and two sons, went to live for a while in the country of Moab."*
> — Ruth 1:1

A famine in the land during Judges prompted a man from Bethlehem who lived in Judah to take his wife and two sons east across the Jordan River to a country called _____.

Throughout the book of Ruth, we hear about the land of "Moab" and "Moabites".

Where does the nation of Moab originate from?

Read Genesis 19:30-38.

_____

_____

_____

_____

_____

The relationship between Israel and Moab was tenuous because of past events.

What events led to the contentious relationship between the two countries?

Numbers 25:1-3

_____

_____

Judges 3:12-13

_____

_____

The Moabites were often who God chose to bring judgment upon the Israelites for their unfaithfulness to Him and His laws. The Israelites harbored bitterness and resentment toward the Moabites for their oppression and abuse toward the Israelites.

Is there someone who has caused you harm or brought pain upon those you love? How do you feel about that person or group of people?

_____

_____

_____

Draw a picture of your facial expression when you think of a particular person or group of people who has wronged you.

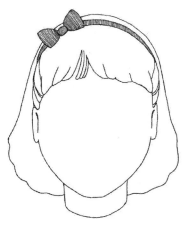

The author of Ruth makes a point to continually bring the reader's attention to Moab and the Moabites throughout the book.

Why do you think the author draws such attention to the foreign nation of Moab?

_____

_____

_____

The story of Ruth is a story of personal redemption but also an introduction to God's ultimate plan to offer salvation to anyone from any tribe or any nation—even our enemies.

How do you feel about God offering forgiveness to someone who has hurt you?

Take some time to communicate your feelings to God about the pain you have experienced and how you truly feel about His compassion toward those who have hurt you or those you love.

_____

_____

_____

_____

_____

_____

_____

_____

Spend time meditating and interacting with Ephesians 4:31-32—

"Get rid of all bitterness, rage and anger, brawling and slander, along with every form of malice. Be kind and compassionate to one another, forgiving each other, just as in Christ God forgave you."

Circle or underline words that stand out to you. Let God's Word speak to you as you concentrate on it.

The Traveling Family

Read Ruth 1:-5

Key Verse:

> *"The man's name was Elimelech, his wife's name was Naomi, and the names of his two sons were Mahlon and Chilion. They were Ephrathites from Bethlehem, Judah. And they went to Moab and lived there."*

—Ruth 1:2

Identify each member of the family who journeyed to the land of Moab.

Husband/Father: _____

Wife/Mother: _____

Son: _____

Son: _____

The name Elimelech means "My God is King."[1]

The name Naomi means "sweetness or pleasantness."[2]

Mahlon and Chilion mean "sickness" and "wasting."[3]

---

[1] "Naomi," Smith's Bible Dictionary, accessed February 19, 2018, https://www.biblestudytools.com/dictionaries/smiths-bible-dictionary/naomi.html.

[2] "Elimelech," Hitchcock's Bible Names Dictionary, accessed February 19, 2018, https://www.biblestudytools.com/dictionaries/hitchcocks-bible-names/elimelech.html

[3] Rev. R. Sinker, "Ruth 1," Ellicott's Commentary for English Readers, accessed February 19, 2018, http://biblehub.com/commentaries/ellicott/ruth/1.htm.

In ancient times, names were given to describe character. With an understanding of the cultural significance of names and the description of each, draw and label each member of the family and how you might imagine each of them.

In yesterday's study, we discovered how the nation of Moab had been instrumental in not only bringing about God's judgment upon the Israelites but also how Moab had led the Israelites away from God.

At this point we have identified the spiritual state of the Israelites and the relationship with Moab.

Based on what you know so far, what is the significance of a man from Bethlehem moving his family to Moab?

_____

_____

Why is it ironic that Elimelech's name means "God is My King"?

_____

_____

Elimelech, a man whose name reflects the authority of God, makes a tragic life-changing decision to take control of his life and the fate of his family by disobeying God.

The author paints Elimelech as a heretic and traitor of God and it is tempting to distance ourselves from someone so tainted.

Yet, I wonder if there are more similarities than we would like to admit.

Have you ever declared God as King of your life but sought to be the ruler of your fate? Explain.

_____

_____

_____

_____

Meditate on Philippians 1:6. Confess your desire and attempt to take charge of your life from the authority of God. Surrender yourself to His work in your life through writing out a prayer below.

_____

_____

_____

_____

_____

_____

_____

_____

_____

_____

_____

_____

Moabite Women

Read Ruth 1:-5

Key verses:

> *Now Elimelech, Naomi's husband, died, and she was left with her two sons. They married Moabite women, one named Orpah and the other Ruth. After they had lived there about ten years,*

> —Ruth 1:3-4

Verse 3 introduces a pivotal point in the story.

According to verse 3, what happened to Naomi's husband?

_____

Draw a picture of Naomi's family based on the information from verse 3.

Verse 4 tells us that Mahlon and Chilion took Moabite women as their wives.

Add their wives to your picture.

Deuteronomy 7:1-5 are the instructions given by Moses (from God) as to how to occupy the Promised Land. God addresses His expectations and requirements for Israel's relationship with foreign nations including marriage.

Read Deuteronomy 7:1-5.

Why did God forbid them from taking foreign spouses?

_____

_____

Foreign spouses introduced foreign/false gods into the homes of God's chosen people.

As Israel conquered the occupying nations of God's Promised Land, they were instructed to wipe out everyone as a way of cleansing and purifying the land.

The two sons of Naomi, Mahlon and Chilion, took wives from Moab.

How is this a reflection of the spiritual status of Israel that we studied in verse 1? (Hint: "In the days when the judges ruled…")

_____

_____

God gave strict instructions for His people as a way of protection.

Are there commands from God's Word that seem excessive or overbearing to you? Give an example.

_____

_____

How might those instructions actually serve to protect you?

_____

_____

_____

Have you neglected some of God's protective instructions and found yourself vulnerable or in a mess? Explain.

_____

_____

Confess your mistake/sin to God. Surrender to His protective commands by committing yourself to His will and ways in your life.

_____

_____

_____

_____

_____

_____

_____

_____

_____

_____

_____

_____

Widows

Read Ruth 1:1-5

Key verses:

> *"They married Moabite women, one named Orpah and the other Ruth. After they had lived there about ten years, both Mahlon and Chilion also died, and Naomi was left without her two sons and her husband."*

> *—Ruth 1:4-5*

How long was the family of Elimelech in Moab before Naomi's husband and sons died?

_____

Naomi's family changed again. Draw a picture of who was left of Naomi's family.

Elimelech left Bethlehem to find a better life for his family.

Did the family find the better life they sought? Explain.

_____

_____

In ancient Israel there were no retirement accounts or welfare safety nets that widowed Naomi could draw from to provide for herself and her daughters-in-law. Nor could she 'go back to work' as a woman today might do.

God had made provisions for widows through His law.

Read Deuteronomy 25:5-10.

Who is a woman to marry if her husband dies?

_____

Even with what was referred to as this "levirate law," Naomi, Ruth, and Orpah have a problem.

They are _____ widows with zero sons or brothers.

What emotions must Naomi and her daughters-in-law have been feeling?

_____

_____

What would come of these women? What hope did they have?

Have you been faced with circumstances that felt hopeless or scary?
Explain.

_____

_____

_____

_____

Have you found yourself fearful of the future? In next week's lesson, we will discover how God begins unfolding His plan for these women.

God didn't email them a report with a detailed agenda but He undoubtedly had one.

Through His Word, God reminds us that we can trust Him. Take some time to meditate on these Scriptures and then share your heart with a loving God who has a plan for you.

Proverbs 3:5-6

Matthew 6:33-34

1 Peter 5:6-7

_____

_____

_____

_____

_____

_____

_____

2

the journey back

notes:

The word *hesed* is translated "kindness, loving-kindness or steadfast love."

notes:

Do nothing out of selfish ambition or vain conceit. Rather, in humility value others above yourselves, not looking to your own interests but each of you to the interests of the others. In your relationships with one another, have the same mindset as Christ Jesus:

Who, being in very nature God, did not consider equality with God something to be used to his own advantage; rather, he made himself nothing by taking the very nature of a servant, being made in human likeness. And being found in appearance as a man, he humbled himself by becoming obedient to death—even death on a cross! —Philippians 2:3-8

Reflection

Given Naomi's situation, if you were her daughter-in-law would you choose to stay with her? Explain.

What do you think compelled Ruth to pledge her loyalty to Naomi?

In your own words explain how Ruth's kindness differs from a casual kindness?

In what ways does your kindness cost you?

The Only Choice

Read Ruth 1:1-7.

Key verses:

> *When Naomi heard in Moab that the LORD had come to the aid of his people by providing food for them, she and her daughters-in-law prepared to return home from there. With her two daughters-in-law she left the place where she had been living and set out on the road that would take them back to the land of Judah.*

> —Ruth 1:6-7

Consider what it must been like to be Naomi. She was devastated by loss and her life had changed dramatically.

Preceding today's passage, how had her life changed? What had she lost?

_____

_____

_____

How many of these events were the result of Naomi's choices?

_____

_____

Naomi went from being a wife and mother to being a widow and lonely mother-in-law in a period of time when her circumstances left her hopeless.

What life-changing events have you experienced that were a result of someone else's choices?

_____

_____

How did you feel about living through the consequences of someone else's actions?

_____

_____

Naomi was overwhelmed when her life in a distant land began to completely unravel.

According to today's passage, what other life-changing events were happening to Naomi?

_____

_____

What moved Naomi to return with her daughters-in-law to her homeland in Judah? (verse 6)

_____

_____

By verse 6, Naomi has become the head of her household. She has two daughters-in-law to consider as well as herself. When she heard conditions had improved in Bethlehem, she returned because she had nowhere else to turn.

Returning to Bethlehem was the right thing to do even if her motive was self-serving and desperate.

There are times we do what is right even when our motives are not the best and that's okay because God uses desperate situations to position us for restoration both with God and others.

Naomi's burden drove her back to where she belonged.

When have you faced a situation so desperate you had no place to turn but God?

_____

_____

Is there something going on your life right now you are trying to handle on your own? Pray and ask God to reveal an area of concern or fear you haven't released to Him.

_____

_____

_____

_____

_____

_____

Too often we wait until the only choice we have left is to return to God before we look to Him for help and healing. Write a prayer of committing your circumstances to God.

_____

_____

_____

_____

_____

_____

Practical Advice

Read Ruth 1:6-18

Key verses:

Then Naomi said to her two daughters-in-law, "Go back, each of you, to your mother's home. May the LORD show you kindness, as you have shown kindness to your dead husbands and to me. May the LORD grant that each of you will find rest in the home of another husband."

Then she kissed them goodbye and they wept aloud and said to her, "We will go back with you to your people."

But Naomi said, "Return home, my daughters. Why would you come with me? Am I going to have any more sons, who could become your husbands? Return home, my daughters; I am too old to have another husband. Even if I thought there was still hope for me—even if I had a husband tonight and then gave birth to sons— would you wait until they grew up? Would you remain unmarried for them? No, my daughters. It is more bitter for me than for you, because the LORD's hand has turned against me!"

—Ruth 1:6-13

The two young widows set out with Naomi for Israel. However, Naomi knew that they would be shunned in Israel.

Why would Naomi assume Ruth and Orpah would be shunned in Israel? (Deuteronomy 23:3)

_____

_____

What did Naomi want Ruth and Orpah to do?

_____

_____

What did Naomi wish for the Lord to grant to Ruth and Orpah?

_____

_____

What does Ruth 1:9 tell us about these three women?

_____

_____

What did Ruth and Orpah offer to do?

_____

_____

Read Deuteronomy 25:5 and Matthew 22:24.

What custom did Naomi refer to?

_____

_____

Naomi's intention was to dissuade the young women by making it clear that if they went with her, they stood no chance of remarriage and children. She had no more sons to offer and likely never would. Furthermore, even if she did, it would be useless, even absurd, for her daughters-in-law to wait for them to grow up.

Naomi's wisdom was logical and practical and left the two young women with a **choice**.

To what else besides family would the young widows have returned?

_____

_____

Have you ever faced a tough choice in the midst of a difficult season? Who helped you through that decision?

_____

_____

_____

_____

James 1:5-8 contrasts a godly wisdom with a worldly wisdom.

Based on the passage in James, what kind of wisdom do you seek?

_____

_____

Which kind of wisdom do you impart on others?

_____

_____

It isn't always easy to discern what is the right or wise choice.

James 1:5 says, *"If any of you lacks wisdom, you should ask God, who gives generously to all without finding fault, and it will be given to you."*

Consider an area in your life where you need wisdom. There may be a sensible choice but is it God's choice?

Take some time to ask God for spirit-filled wisdom.

_____

_____

_____

_____

_____

_____

_____

_____

_____

_____

Week 2, Day 3

God Is Not Finished with Your Story

Read Ruth 1:11-18

Key verses:

> *But Ruth replied, "Don't urge me to leave you or to turn back from you. Where you go I will go, and where you stay I will stay. Your people will be my people and your God my God. Where you die I will die, and there I will be buried. May the LORD deal with me, be it ever so severely, if even death separates you and me." When Naomi realized that Ruth was determined to go with her, she stopped urging her.*
>
> —Ruth 1:16-18

How did Orpah react to Naomi's request?

_____

_____

How did Ruth react to Naomi's request?

_____

_____

Naomi tried to reason with Ruth. She too could have gone back as Orpah had done, to her people and her gods. Ruth weighed the matter and considered the consequences. The Scriptures record that Ruth clung to Naomi.

Ruth's answer to her mother-in-law speaks to something spiritually significant that has happened in the life of Ruth.

Do you think of converts happening in the Old Testament time or does that seem like only a New Testament event?

_____

_____

Who are some other non-Israelite followers of God?

_____ (Numbers 23:12, Joshua 14:14)

_____ (Joshua 2:1, 6:25, Matthew 1:5)

_____ (Jonah 1:13-16)

Paul discussed the process of "grafting in" non-Israelites (or Gentiles) through the new covenant of Jesus in Romans 9-11, but God was grafting in non-Israelites even before the New Testament.

By committing herself to Naomi, Ruth was committing herself to Naomi's God.

For how long did Ruth pledge herself to Naomi and Naomi's God?

_____

_____

What did Ruth turn away from in order to devote herself to a new life with Naomi?

_____

_____

Ruth was not only walking away from the idolatrous nation of Moab, she was walking away from apparent security into an unknown future. Ruth was demonstrating what Hebrews 11:1 describes as faith.

"Now faith is confidence in what we hope for and assurance about what we do not see."

Verse 18 describes Ruth as "determined."

What part does determination play in your spiritual walk with God?

_____

_____

_____

_____

Consider Ruth's commitment to Naomi and Naomi's God. Ruth has entered into a covenant relationship with Naomi and God—meaning she's sticking with her NO MATTER WHAT.

Is there a relationship God has led you to that is anything but easy? Is God asking you to persevere with someone by committing to sticking it out even when it gets messy? Talk to God about this relationship and your feelings. Ask Him for wisdom and determination to obey Him by faith.

_____

_____

_____

_____

_____

_____

_____

_____

_____

_____

Home Sweet Home

Read Ruth 1:18-22

Key verses:

When Naomi realized that Ruth was determined to go with her, she stopped urging her. So the two women went on until they came to Bethlehem. When they arrived in Bethlehem, the whole town was stirred because of them, and the women exclaimed, "Can this be Naomi?"

"Don't call me Naomi," she told them. "Call me Mara, because the Almighty has made my life very bitter. I went away full, but the LORD has brought me back empty. Why call me Naomi? The LORD has afflicted me; the Almighty has brought misfortune upon me."

—Ruth 1:18-21

Draw a picture of what is left of Naomi's family at this point in the story.

Verse 18 says, "When Naomi realized that Ruth was determined to go with her, she stopped urging her." The literal Hebrew translation of "she stopped urging her" is "She stopped talking to her."[4]

---

4 HCSB Study Bible Notes

How do you picture the journey for Naomi and Ruth as they traveled to Bethlehem?

_____

_____

As they arrived into Bethlehem, how was Naomi received?

_____

_____

Verse 19 says, "the whole town was stirred because of them." The city buzzed at Naomi's return.

How do you picture the scene as Naomi and Ruth arrived into town?

_____

_____

Who is pointedly ignored in this scene? Why do you think that is?

_____

_____

Without the benefit of social media or email, what questions must the townspeople have been asking surrounding the return of Naomi?

_____

_____

One woman actually (because there is always someone who will usually say what everyone else is thinking) said aloud, "Can this be Naomi?"

Why might this outspoken woman ask such a question?

_____

_____

As Naomi returns to Bethlehem, she comes as one who is humiliated. She left Bethlehem with a husband and sons but returns with only a foreign daughter-in-law. She was not returning with her head high and a highlight reel of pleasant memories. She returns as a broken woman to be pitied.

In tomorrow's homework we will examine Naomi's attitude as she returned but as we conclude today's homework, let's seek to understand what it was like to be Naomi under these circumstances.

Have you ever experienced humiliation that left you embarrassed and ashamed? Explain.

_____

_____

What did you do? Did you hide? Where did you turn? What was your response to humiliation?

_____

_____

_____

_____

Scripture tells us that Jesus willingly humiliated Himself by coming as a baby to eventually hang naked upon a cross for our sins. (Phil. 2:6-8)

Considering your own humiliation, can you imagine willingly choosing it?

Record your thoughts and offer your thankfulness to Jesus for sacrificing His dignity so you might enjoy participating as an heir of God in His Kingdom work.

_____

_____

_____

_____

_____

_____

_____

_____

_____

_____

_____

_____

_____

_____

_____

_____

Week 2, Day 5

Bitterness Revealed

Read Ruth 1:6-22

Key verses:

> *"Don't call me Naomi," she told them. "Call me Mara, because the*
> *Almighty has made my life very bitter. I went away full, but*
> *the LORD has brought me back empty. Why call me Naomi?*
> *The LORD has afflicted me; the Almighty has brought misfortune*
> *upon me."*

> —Ruth 1:20-21

When Naomi returns home she wants to be called "Mara" which means "bitter one."[5] "Naomi" means pleasant and lovely but as she returns to her home in Bethlehem, surrounded by her friends and the people of God, she urges them to refer to her as "bitter."

What is Naomi's attitude in the midst of tragedy and loss?

_____

_____

Naomi is bitter. Bitterness always distorts our perspective. In Naomi's case, bitterness led to blame. Without being insensitive, let's consider how Naomi got here.

Who moved from Bethlehem to Moab?

_____

_____

---

[5] Jerry Gifford, "The Burden and Bitterness of a Barren Life," accessed February 19, 2018, http://www.lifeway.com/Article/sermon-ruth-burden-bitterness-barenness-joy-fulfillment.

Yet, who does Naomi blame? (verses 13, 20 & 21)

_____

Bitterness also led Naomi to hostility and negativity.

In verses 15-18, Ruth declares her allegiance and faithful love to Naomi.

What appreciation for Ruth and her steadfast devotion do you notice by Naomi's attitude throughout the remainder of the chapter?

_____

_____

If you were Ruth, how would you feel?

_____

_____

What was it that Naomi in her grief could not see?

_____

_____

In the midst of terrible circumstances, it is easy to lose perspective and stop trusting God.

Have you found yourself in a situation when God seemed distant?

_____

_____

Bitterness often begins with a matter of unforgiveness. Hebrews 12:14-15 urges believers to live at peace with one another in order to squelch bitterness that draws you away from God.

Is there someone (even God) who you harbor resentment and an unforgiving heart toward?

_____

_____

How has bitterness caused you to miss God at work in your life?

_____

_____

God wasn't done with Naomi's story but she couldn't see it because her heart was wracked with bitterness and blame.

God isn't done with your story either. Confess bitterness and resentment to God and determine in your heart to trust Him (just as Ruth did) with the remainder of your story. Because just as with Ruth and Naomi, there is more to your story. Trust God to write it.

_____

_____

_____

_____

_____

_____

_____

_____

_____

_____

_____

_____

3

it just so happened

notes:

Commit to the Lord whatever you do, and he will establish your plans.—Proverbs 16:3

notes:

Reflection

How do you feel about coincidence versus God's divine intervention?

How are you changed by recognizing God's intervention in your life in the "it just so happened" moments?

When have you found yourself in the thick of "surviving" while anticipating with hope God's plan to redeem a trying season?

A Man Named Boaz

Read Ruth 2:1-23

Key verses:

> *Now Naomi had a relative on her husband's side, a man of standing from the clan of Elimelech, whose name was Boaz. And Ruth the Moabite said to Naomi, "Let me go to the fields and pick up the leftover grain behind anyone in whose eyes I find favor." Naomi said to her, "Go ahead, my daughter." So she went out, entered a field and began to glean behind the harvesters. As it turned out, she was working in a field belonging to Boaz, who was from the clan of Elimelech. Just then Boaz arrived from Bethlehem and greeted the harvesters, "The LORD be with you!" "The LORD bless you!" they answered.*

> —Ruth 2:1-4

What do you learn about Boaz in verse 1?

_____

_____

Boaz is described as a man of "standing" in the New International Version. In other versions of Scripture, he is described as "a man of prominence," "a worthy man," and "a man of great wealth and influence."

By the description of Boaz's interaction with his employees how else might you describe Boaz?

_____

What kind of relationship does it appear Boaz has with his employees?

_____

_____

What did Ruth request of Naomi?

_____

_____

Describe Ruth's plan to take care of her mother-in-law?

_____

_____

_____

_____

What traits of Ruth's character do you see in her plan?

_____

_____

Why did Ruth think she might find someone to let her glean from their field? (See Leviticus 19:9-10, 23:22 and Deuteronomy 24:19-22)

_____

_____

God was providing for Naomi and Ruth long before they ever had a need. God was orchestrating the details for their redemption and rescue before they were able to see His hand at work.

Verse 3 uses the wording, "As it turned out..." or in some translations "And she happened...."

What does the wording in this verse show us about God's clear and directive hand in this story?

_____

_____

What do you notice about the intersection of God's sovereignty at work with human responsibility?

_____

_____

Look up Proverbs 16:9 and write it below.

_____

_____

Have you experienced God's detailed provision in your own life? Explain.

_____

_____

In what way today do you need the reminder that God is in control?

_____

_____

Journal a prayer declaring God's sovereign control in your life. Proclaim His kindness and goodness and declare your trust in His plan to redeem your story even if you can't see it yet.

_____

_____

_____

_____

_____

_____

_____

_____

_____

_____

_____

_____

_____

_____

_____

_____

_____

_____

A Safe Refuge

Read Ruth 2:1-23

Key verses:

Boaz asked the overseer of his harvesters, "Who does that young woman belong to?" The overseer replied, "She is the Moabite who came back from Moab with Naomi. She said, 'Please let me glean and gather among the sheaves behind the harvesters.' She came into the field and has remained here from morning till now, except for a short rest in the shelter."

So Boaz said to Ruth, "My daughter, listen to me. Don't go and glean in another field and don't go away from here. Stay here with the women who work for me. Watch the field where the men are harvesting, and follow along after the women. I have told the men not to lay a hand on you. And whenever you are thirsty, go and get a drink from the water jars the men have filled."

At this, she bowed down with her face to the ground. She asked him, "Why have I found such favor in your eyes that you notice me—a foreigner?" Boaz replied, "I've been told all about what you have done for your mother-in-law since the death of your husband—how you left your father and mother and your homeland and came to live with a people you did not know before. May the LORD repay you for what you have done. May you be richly rewarded by the LORD, the God of Israel, under whose wings you have come to take refuge."

"May I continue to find favor in your eyes, my lord," she said. "You have put me at ease by speaking kindly to your servant—though I do not have the standing of one of your servants."

—Ruth 2:5-13

What did Boaz ask?

_____

_____

What did the servant tell Boaz about Ruth?

_____

_____

What did Ruth request of Boaz?

_____

_____

How did Boaz respond?

_____

What special kindness does Boaz show to Ruth and why?

_____

_____

_____

_____

Boaz showed favor far beyond the requirements of the law. Provisions for the poor, sojourners, widows, and orphans allowed them to gather standing grain in corners or borders of a field as well as dropped stalks and left behind sheaves (recall Lev. 19:9-10, 23:22 and Deut. 24:19). Boaz went beyond his obligatory duty in order to care for Ruth.

In Boaz's expression of love through his compassion and generous spirit, we catch a glimpse of the love of God. Like Ruth, we too have been welcomed by God when we did nothing to deserve His kindness.

The most important question Ruth asks in this passage is in verse 10.

What question does Ruth ask of Boaz?

_____

_____

It might seem Boaz's answer is found in verse 11 regarding Ruth's treatment of Naomi. But the real answer is found in verse 12, where Boaz said that she had come to take refuge under the wings of the God of Israel.

What do you think a "refuge" is?

_____

_____

Look up Psalm 46:1 and write it below.

_____

_____

Describe what "taking refuge under the wings of the Lord" looks like in your life.

_____

_____

_____

_____

In written communication, share with God the significance of Him as your refuge and strength, an ever-present help in times of trouble. Lean into the truth of His protection today.

_____

_____

_____

_____

_____

_____

_____

_____

_____

_____

_____

_____

_____

_____

_____

_____

_____

_____

_____

_____

_____

_____

Week 3, Day 3

Undeserved Favor

Read Ruth 2:1-23

Key verses:

> At mealtime Boaz said to her, "Come over here. Have some bread and dip it in the wine vinegar."
>
> When she sat down with the harvesters, he offered her some roasted grain. She ate all she wanted and had some left over. As she got up to glean, Boaz gave orders to his men, "Let her gather among the sheaves and don't reprimand her. Even pull out some stalks for her from the bundles and leave them for her to pick up, and don't rebuke her."
>
> So Ruth gleaned in the field until evening. Then she threshed the barley she had gathered, and it amounted to about an ephah. She carried it back to town, and her mother-in-law saw how much she had gathered. Ruth also brought out and gave her what she had left over after she had eaten enough.
>
> Her mother-in-law asked her, "Where did you glean today? Where did you work? Blessed be the man who took notice of you!"
>
> Then Ruth told her mother-in-law about the one at whose place she had been working. "The name of the man I worked with today is Boaz," she said.
>
> —Ruth 2:14-19

Describe the meal that Ruth and Boaz shared.

_____

_____

At mealtime, Boaz paid special attention to Ruth in sight of the other workers. This was important for her protection.

As he left, he gave special instructions in regards to Ruth. What were they?

_____

_____

The King James Version translates verse 16 this way, "And let fall also some of the **handfuls on purpose** for her, and leave them, that she may glean them, and rebuke her not." (emphasis added)

The "handfuls on purpose" is a beautiful picture of mercy and lavish grace. As Boaz's workers purposely let extra grain fall for Ruth, so God often lays unexpected blessings in our paths. Sometimes our prayers are answered far beyond our expectations and other times when we have about given up on our prayers being answered God intervenes in surprisingly wonderful ways.

When have you experienced God's undeserved favor in your life?

_____

_____

Describe Ruth's work ethic.

_____

_____

Ruth worked from sun up to sun down while Naomi was back in Bethlehem waiting and wondering.

What thoughts and emotions do you think Naomi experienced while Ruth was away?

_____

_____

What did Ruth bring home that day to Naomi?

_____

_____

An **ephah** of barley would have been the equivalent of a half of a bushel or about five gallons of barley.[6]

When Ruth returned with unexpected provision, what did Naomi want to know?

_____

_____

How did Naomi respond to Boaz's provision?

_____

_____

I picture Ruth and Naomi staying somewhere bleak, possibly in a cave, because they were destitute without any financial means. They were grief-stricken, weary from travels and hungry. Ruth and Naomi have had to be patient and wait for God's timing. When Ruth left Naomi to seek food through gleaning, I wonder if Naomi allowed herself to hope for what Ruth might bring when she returned.

When have you had to be patient and wait for God's timing? Were you hope-filled or full of doubt?

_____

_____

_____

_____

---

[6] Discipler's Bible Study, Judges/Ruth, p.19

God is always writing your story. There are chapters that are painful and hard and there are others that seem more carefree and full of promise. No matter what chapter you are in, God is not done with your story. There is more to come.

Talk to God about the season of life you are walking through. Share with Him your doubts and your hopes. Surrender each chapter to Him and intentionally choose to trust He is not done with you. (Phil. 1:6)

_____

_____

_____

_____

_____

_____

_____

_____

_____

_____

_____

_____

_____

_____

_____

_____

An Uncommon Kindness

Read Ruth 2:1-23

Key verses:

The LORD bless him!" Naomi said to her daughter-in-law. "He has not stopped showing his kindness to the living and the dead." She added, "That man is our close relative; he is one of our guardian-redeemers."

Then Ruth the Moabite said, "He even said to me, 'Stay with my workers until they finish harvesting all my grain.'"

Naomi said to Ruth her daughter-in-law, "It will be good for you, my daughter, to go with the women who work for him, because in someone else's field you might be harmed."

So Ruth stayed close to the women of Boaz to glean until the barley and wheat harvests were finished. And she lived with her mother-in-law.

—Ruth 2:20-23

Naomi said, "He has not stopped showing his kindness to the living and the dead."

Who is the "He" Naomi refers to in the statement above? (Hint: It isn't Boaz.)

_____

What attribute of God did Naomi mention?

_____

How is this attribute seen in the following passages?

Romans 8:32

_____

_____

2 Corinthians 8:9

_____

_____

Titus 3:4-7

_____

_____

Which of these evidences of kindness have you experienced? Explain.

_____

_____

What did Ruth find out about Boaz that she did not know?

_____

_____

Verse 20 is the first mention of a kinsman-redeemer in the story. It is a key word and concept originating from Leviticus 25:25. As part of the legal system, a kinsman-redeemer was a "savior" figure or one who was responsible for coming to the rescue of the needy.

Look up Leviticus 25:25 and write it below.

_____

_____

What advice does Naomi give Ruth that echoes Boaz's instructions?

_____

_____

Naomi immediately saw God's hand at work. When once Naomi was bitter, now she is grateful.

Do you acknowledge God's goodness and kindness or are you bitter at life's hard places? Explain.

_____

_____

Pause now and think of examples of God's kindness to you. What do you find to be grateful for?

_____

_____

_____

_____

> *But when the kindness and love of God our Savior appeared, he saved us, not because of righteous things we had done, but because of his mercy. He saved us through the washing of rebirth and renewal by the Holy Spirit, whom he poured out on us generously through Jesus Christ our Savior, so that, having been justified by his grace, we might become heirs having the hope of eternal life.*

—Titus 3:4-7

Meditate on the passage from Titus. As you meditate on the Scripture, underline or circle words that stand out to you. Make notes on the following page about the significance of God's lovingkindness to you.

Thank God for His kindness and ask Him to show you how He is at work in your story today.

_____

_____

_____

_____

_____

_____

_____

_____

_____

_____

_____

_____

_____

_____

Mama's Boy

Read Joshua 2:1-7 and Matthew 1:5

Key verse:

> *Salmon the father of Boaz, whose mother was Rahab, Boaz the father of Obed, whose mother was Ruth, Obed the father of Jesse,*

> —Matthew 1:5

Boaz is the son of: _____ and _____.

The background of Boaz might not seem significant but it is! I get so excited about how God chose to intertwine the stories of two women who by all logic should never have crossed paths nor been brought into His family.

During our time of study in week 2, you might remember this question:

> *Who are some other non-Israelite followers of God?*

I led you through multiple passages of Scripture to identify Old Testament converts.

Two passages we looked at were Joshua 2:1 and 6:25.

Who was the woman mentioned in the verses in Joshua?

_____

According to Joshua 2:1, who was Rahab? What did she do for a living?

_____

Before there was a Ruth and before there was a Boaz, there were Israelites wondering in the wilderness waiting for the day God would allow them into the Promised Land.

A man by the name of Joshua led the Israelites and decided to send two spies to check out the land and report back.

When the two men entered the town of Jericho they came to the house of _____.

Rahab hid the spies from the king and in exchange for her loyalty asked for mercy for herself and her family when the Israelites returned to take over the city.

But Joshua spared Rahab the prostitute, with her family and all who belonged to her, because she hid the men Joshua had sent as spies to Jericho—and she lives among the Israelites to this day.—Joshua 6:25

Look up Hebrews 11:31 and write it below:

_____

_____

_____

Though Rahab married an Israelite and bore a son, she herself was not an Israelite. Rahab was also a prostitute before she came to live among the Israelites.

How do you think Rahab was treated by the other Israelite women? Explain.

_____

_____

What might Boaz have observed about the treatment of his foreign mother as he grew up?

_____

_____

How do you think having Rahab as a mother would have shaped the attitude Boaz had toward a foreigner like Ruth?

_____

_____

_____

Long before Elimelech sojourned to Moab and Ruth joined his family, God was shaping the life of a young man who would redeem Ruth and her mother-in-law.

God had gone ahead of Ruth and was shaping the sum of not only her experiences but the experiences of a man named Boaz by putting him in a family with a very specific woman for a very specific reason.

> *The LORD himself goes before you and will be with you; he will never leave you nor forsake you. Do not be afraid; do not be discouraged.—Deuteronomy 31:8*

As women, we often consider the emotional impact painful situations have on those that we love. We are concerned for our children, our grandchildren or those that we are closest to.

We need to be reminded that God knows where each of us are. He has a plan for the sum of our experiences—even the painful ones.

Take some time to meditate on Deuteronomy 31:8 and talk to God about your fears and concerns and then choose to trust He is at work in ways you can't begin to imagine because there is more to your story that you don't even know about.

_____

_____

_____

_____

_____

_____

_____

_____

_____

4

that was awkward

notes:

Notes:

"For I know the plans I have for you declares the Lord, plans to prosper you and not to harm you—plans to give you a hope and a future."— Jeremiah 29:11

Reflection

When have you experienced God asking you to do something that risked your dignity and had the potential (or even turned out to be) socially awkward or embarrassing?

How does the risk of embarrassment or rejection cause you to resist obeying God's leading in your life?

What makes taking a risk with God different than taking other risks?

Naomi's Concern

Read Ruth 3

Key verses:

> One day Ruth's mother-in-law Naomi said to her, "My daughter, I must find a home for you, where you will be well provided for. Now Boaz, with whose women you have worked, is a relative of ours. Tonight he will be winnowing barley on the threshing floor.
>
> —Ruth 3:1-2

Whose best interest did Naomi have in mind?

_____

According to the passage, what is Naomi's concern for Ruth?

_____

_____

Ruth 2:23 says, "So Ruth stayed close to the women of Boaz to glean until the barley and wheat harvests were finished. And she lived with her mother-in-law."

As the barley and wheat harvests came to an end, what dilemma faced Ruth and Naomi?

_____

_____

A lack of long-term provision concerned Naomi and she determined it was time to seek after a more permanent solution.

Naomi reminded Ruth that Boaz was not only a kind field owner that allowed her to glean but was also what?

_____

Though Ruth had already told Naomi, "Your God will be my God," as a Moabite, Ruth was not accustomed to the new laws of marriage that the Israelites abided by.

By reminding Ruth of Boaz's relationship with their family, what was Naomi also explaining to Ruth? (Hint: Leviticus 25:25)

_____

_____

What plans did Boaz have for the evening?

_____

_____

According to the Holman Christian Standard Bible Study notes,

> "At the end of the barley harvest, in late May or June, the barley had to be winnowed, tossed into the air with a fork allowing the wind to carry away the lighter chaff while the heavier grain fell to the ground. At night someone would guard the grain against being stolen or eaten by animals. Apparently this was Boaz's night to be on duty."[7]

Verses 1 and 2 place the characters of our story where?

Ruth and Naomi: _____

Boaz: _____

---

[7] HCSB Study Bible Notes, Ruth 3:1-3, p.436

Describe how you picture the scene of Ruth and Naomi.

_____

_____

_____

_____

Describe how you picture Boaz as he winnowed the barley.

_____

_____

_____

_____

Naomi showed concern for Ruth and her future well-being. When have you been concerned for your loved ones?

_____

_____

_____

_____

What kind of conversation did you have with them regarding your concerns?

_____

_____

_____

_____

As you consider the future for yourself and those you care about, take some time to have a conversation with God about how you feel. Meditate on Jeremiah 29:11 and commit your heart to trusting God for His plan over your own.

_____

_____

_____

_____

_____

_____

_____

_____

_____

_____

_____

_____

A Bold Plan

Read Ruth 3

Key verses:

Wash, put on perfume, and get dressed in your best clothes. Then go down to the threshing floor, but don't let him know you are there until he has finished eating and drinking. When he lies down, note the place where he is lying. Then go and uncover his feet and lie down. He will tell you what to do."

"I will do whatever you say," Ruth answered.

—Ruth 3:3-5

What advice did Naomi give to Ruth?

_____

_____

How was Ruth to get Boaz to notice her?

_____

_____

The New American Standard Bible translates verse 3 this way,

> *"Wash yourself therefore, and anoint yourself and put on your best clothes, and go down to the threshing floor; but do not make yourself known to the man until he has finished eating and drinking."*

Naomi instructs Ruth to "anoint herself" presumably with fine oils to be more presentable and attractive.

Look up 2 Samuel 14:2. Besides becoming more attractive, what else might Naomi have been suggesting to Ruth by instructing her to anoint herself?

_____

_____

_____

_____

How did Ruth react to the advice of Naomi?

_____

_____

What is your first impression of Naomi's advice to Ruth?

_____

_____

This is not the first time we have seen Naomi give advice to Ruth in our story. What advice had Naomi given to Ruth previously? (Ruth 1:8-13)

_____

_____

How did Ruth respond to Naomi's previous advice?

_____

_____

Why do you think Ruth's response to Naomi is different this time?

_____

_____

_____

_____

How do you think the dynamics of Ruth and Naomi's relationship might have changed over the course of their time in Bethlehem? Explain.

_____

_____

_____

_____

Naomi formulated a strange plan (even for Old Testament times) for Ruth in order to provide her with security.

When have you made plans for someone else in order to meet their needs or fix their problem? How did your plans turn out?

_____

_____

_____

_____

God is writing each of our stories as part of His big story. No matter how vexed you may feel about the circumstances in your life or the lives of those you love, the story isn't over. God is still at work.

Take some time to talk to God about the story He is writing for your life or the life of someone you love. Ask Him questions, share with Him your impatience and confusion and then meditate on

Isaiah 55: 8-9:

> *"For my thoughts are not your thoughts,*
> *neither are your ways my ways,"*
> *declares the Lord.*
> *"As the heavens are higher than the earth,*
> *so are my ways higher than your ways*
> *and my thoughts than your thoughts."*

_____

_____

_____

_____

_____

_____

_____

_____

_____

_____

_____

_____

_____

_____

Week 4, Day 3

A Surprise Guest

Read Ruth 3

Key verses:

> *So she went down to the threshing floor and did everything her mother-in-law told her to do. When Boaz had finished eating and drinking and was in good spirits, he went over to lie down at the far end of the grain pile. Ruth approached quietly, uncovered his feet and lay down. In the middle of the night something startled the man; he turned—and there was a woman lying at his feet!*
>
> *"Who are you?" he asked.*
>
> *"I am your servant Ruth," she said. "Spread the corner of your garment over me, since you are a guardian-redeemer of our family."*
>
> —Ruth 3:6-9

After "freshening up," Ruth ventured down to the threshing floor. The threshing floor was usually a place outside of town where the harvesters could winnow their barley.

Winnowing was hard work and after a long day, what did Boaz do?

_____

_____

While Boaz ate and drank, Ruth would have been waiting for Boaz to fall asleep in order to carry out Naomi's instructions.

What might have been going through Ruth's mind as she waited?

_____

_____

How are you waiting on God right now? What thoughts flood your mind as you wait?

_____

_____

The New International Version says that Ruth approached how?

_____

How do you picture Ruth as she entered the threshing floor in the middle of the night?

_____

_____

What place did Ruth take on the threshing floor?

_____

_____

What time did Boaz wake up?

_____

What did Boaz ask Ruth when he was awakened in the middle of the night?

_____

What do you imagine was running through Boaz's mind when he discovered a woman lying at his feet?

_____

_____

*Did Ruth follow **all** the advice of her mother-in-law? Explain.*

_____

_____

Naomi anticipated Boaz taking the initiative in the conversation, yet Ruth responded to Boaz's question about her identity by stating her purpose.

What did Ruth ask of Boaz when he discovered her at his feet?

_____

_____

This was Ruth's formal request for Boaz to carry out his duty of the kinsman-redeemer under the law (Leviticus 25:25 and Deuteronomy 25:5-6). It was also a marriage proposal.

Though Ruth had a just claim on Boaz as a close relative or kinsmen redeemer, she was bold in her request.

The Hebrew word for the kinsman-redeemer is "go-el" and used by Job in Job 19:25, *"I know that my redeemer lives, and that in the end he will stand on the earth."*

Boaz is a picture of the relationship we have with Christ as our redeemer. We are destitute and helpless without someone to come and "buy" us back for the Father when we were lost through the penalty of death for our sin.

Just as Ruth boldly came to Boaz to be redeemed, we too have the opportunity to boldly come to Jesus for redemption—both for our salvation and our current circumstances.

"Therefore let us approach the throne of grace with boldness, so that we may receive mercy and find grace to help us at the proper time."

—Hebrews 4:16 (HCSB)

Have you asked Jesus to redeem your life? Explain.

_____

_____

Spend some time thanking God for His redeeming work in your life. Commit your trust in Him for His plan for the rest of your story.

_____

_____

_____

_____

_____

_____

_____

_____

_____

_____

_____

A Honorable Pair

Read Ruth 3

Key verses:

"The LORD bless you, my daughter," he replied. "This kindness is greater than that which you showed earlier: You have not run after the younger men, whether rich or poor. And now, my daughter, don't be afraid. I will do for you all you ask. All the people of my town know that you are a woman of noble character. Although it is true that I am a guardian-redeemer of our family, there is another who is more closely related than I. Stay here for the night, and in the morning if he wants to do his duty as your guardian-redeemer, good; let him redeem you. But if he is not willing, as surely as the LORD lives I will do it. Lie here until morning."

So she lay at his feet until morning, but got up before anyone could be recognized; and he said, "No one must know that a woman came to the threshing floor."

He also said, "Bring me the shawl you are wearing and hold it out." When she did so, he poured into it six measures of barley and placed the bundle on her. Then he went back to town.

—Ruth 3:10-15

Did Boaz understand Ruth's request of him? Explain.

_____

_____

What impressed Boaz about Ruth?

_____

_____

Boaz may have been considerably older than Ruth. He commended her for not encouraging younger or wealthier men.

What did Boaz agree to do for Ruth?

_____

_____

What did everyone in town know about Ruth?

_____

_____

Ruth is described as a woman of "noble character." What evidences of Ruth's character throughout the story confirm such a description?

_____

_____

_____

_____

After commending Ruth for her behavior, Boaz brings up a problem. What was the one problem that needed to be handled?

_____

_____

As we seek to follow God in obedience, we are almost always met with obstacles and resistance. When have you sought to be obedient to God and discovered obstacles to carry out your obedience?

_____

_____

_____

_____

How did Boaz reassure Ruth?

_____

_____

How was the integrity of Boaz shown in these verses?

_____

_____

What did Boaz give to Ruth?

_____

_____

This part of Ruth's story is such a beautiful picture of two people seeking to honor God and each other with their actions. Ruth and Boaz lived in a culture similar to the one we find ourselves where integrity and honor towards God and others is rare.

Spend some time asking God how you can honor Him in your relationships by protecting and sacrificing for someone else.

_____

_____

_____

_____

_____

_____

Waiting in Peace

Read Ruth 3

Key verses:

When Ruth came to her mother-in-law, Naomi asked, "How did it go, my daughter?" Then she told her everything Boaz had done for her and added, "He gave me these six measures of barley, saying, 'Don't go back to your mother-in-law empty-handed.'" Then Naomi said, "Wait, my daughter, until you find out what happens. For the man will not rest until the matter is settled today."

—Ruth 3:16-18

After discreetly leaving the threshing floor, Ruth arrived at home with the load of grain and a wonderful story to tell.

What did Naomi say about the gift from Boaz?

_____

_____

The King James Version reads,

> *Then said she, Sit still, my daughter, until thou know how the matter will fall: for the man will not be in rest, until he have finished the thing this day. (Ruth 3:18)*

After such an exciting night and a huge development in the story, why would Naomi instruct Ruth to "sit still"?

_____

_____

Ruth and Naomi had done their part, now it was completely out of their control. All they could do was wait.

Naomi and Ruth were waiting on both Boaz and the Lord.

When have you done everything in your own power to accomplish a particular outcome but reached a place where the actual result was completely out of your control? (i.e. parenting)

_____

_____

Were you anxious or at peace? Explain.

_____

_____

Some matters we take to the Lord and leave with Him, knowing there is nothing more we can do. We rest in the Lord, confident that He is busy acting on our behalf.

What does Scripture tell us about God's activity even in the midst of waiting?

Psalm 121:4_____

_____

John 5:17_____

_____

Philippians 1:6_____

_____

It isn't always easy to wait especially if we want so badly to control the outcome of a situation. Often, waiting can lead to anxiety and fear.

When our minds are prone to anxiousness, how does the Bible tell us we can find peace?

Isaiah 26:3_____

_____

Philippians 4:6_____

_____

Proverbs 3:5-6_____

_____

Armed with the truth of Scripture and a reminder of God's activity and character, will you wait in faith and trust while God works out the details of your faith and trust in Him?

_____

_____

Talk to God about your inclination towards anxiety when you lack control of a situation. Declare to Him your desire and commitment to rest in His plan for your life.

_____

_____

_____

_____

_____

_____

_____

_____

5

a long time coming

notes:

notes:

But because of his great love for us, God, who is rich in mercy, made us alive with Christ even when we were dead in transgressions—it is by grace you have been saved. —Ephesians 2:4-5

Reflection

When have you or someone you know endured through a difficult season and were able to rejoice when hopes were finally realized?

When have you experienced seasons of endurance that ended much differently than you hoped or expected?

How can you look back and see God working out His plan despite circumstances you never would have chosen for yourself?

The Town Gate

Read Ruth 4

Key verses:

Meanwhile Boaz went up to the town gate and sat down there just as the guardian-redeemer he had mentioned came along. Boaz said, "Come over here, my friend, and sit down." So he went over and sat down.

Boaz took ten of the elders of the town and said, "Sit here," and they did so.

—Ruth 4:1-2

Why did Boaz go to the gate of the city?

_____

_____

In the following verses, what significance does "the gate" have?

*Joshua 20:4*_____

_____

*1 Kings 22:10*_____

_____

*2 Samuel 15:2*_____

_____

*Proverbs 31:23 and 31*_____

_____

The town gate was a place to conduct business. Daily, men would come to bring their cases for discussion and resolution. We might compare a city gate to city hall or a county courthouse.

Who came "just as" Boaz sat at the gate?

_____

_____

The writer of Ruth seems surprised by the swiftness of events as the very person who was most crucial to the proceedings at this point appeared "just as" Boaz arrived at the gate.

When have we seen it "just so happen" before in the story of Ruth? (Ruth 2:3)

_____

_____

Do you think it was pure chance or God's hand at work in Ruth's story? Explain.

_____

_____

It is true that the close relative may have come purely by chance but we don't serve a God who works in coincidences. Ascribing glory to chance instead of to God Himself lacks spiritual sight when happenstance coincides with God's will and purpose.

How many men did Boaz invite to sit down with him at the gate?

_____

What name is given for the guardian-redeemer?

_____

Why do you think he is left unnamed?

_____

_____

Boaz's actions in response to Ruth's request of him in chapter 3 are being carried out in these first verses of chapter 4. The tragic events and days of perseverance have led to this scene.

When have you experienced turning point moments in your own life that you believed might never come during seasons of grief or endurance?

_____

_____

Is there a turning point moment you were hoping right now for this season of your life? Explain.

_____

_____

_____

Write the words of Hebrews 11:1 below.

_____

_____

Talk to God about your hopes for the future and commit your faith in His plan for what is ahead.

_____

_____

_____

_____

Unwilling

Read Ruth 4

Key verses:

Then he said to the guardian-redeemer, "Naomi, who has come back from Moab, is selling the piece of land that belonged to our relative Elimelech. I thought I should bring the matter to your attention and suggest that you buy it in the presence of these seated here and in the presence of the elders of my people. If you will redeem it, do so. But if you will not, tell me, so I will know. For no one has the right to do it except you, and I am next in line."

"I will redeem it," he said.

Then Boaz said, "On the day you buy the land from Naomi, you also acquire Ruth the Moabite, the dead man's widow, in order to maintain the name of the dead with his property." At this, the guardian-redeemer said, "Then I cannot redeem it because I might endanger my own estate. You redeem it yourself. I cannot do it."

—Ruth 4:3-6

What did Boaz explain to the close relative about Naomi?

_____

_____

What did Boaz ask him to do?

_____

_____

What additional information did Boaz then add?

_____

_____

What description of Ruth did Boaz include?

_____

_____

Why do you think he included this detail?

_____

_____

What was the close relative's response to the additional information given to him by Boaz?

_____

_____

Boaz was methodical in his release of information. He took the 'close-relative' on a journey of first wanting to redeem Naomi's land to refusing.

Why do you think he refused?

_____

_____

Compare the close relative's willingness to redeem Naomi's land and her husband's name and Boaz's willingness.

_____

_____

The close-relative was not only unwilling to redeem Naomi and Ruth, he claimed his inability to redeem them.

Write 2 Corinthians 8:12 below.

_____

_____

How does this verse challenge our excuses for carrying out the assignments given to us by God?

_____

_____

Spend time talking to God about your willingness and trusting Him with all you have to offer.

_____

_____

_____

_____

_____

_____

_____

_____

_____

_____

_____

Reason to Rejoice

Read Ruth 4

Key passage:

(Now in earlier times in Israel, for the redemption and transfer of property to become final, one party took off his sandal and gave it to the other. This was the method of legalizing transactions in Israel.)

So the guardian-redeemer said to Boaz, "Buy it yourself." And he removed his sandal. Then Boaz announced to the elders and all the people, "Today you are witnesses that I have bought from Naomi all the property of Elimelech, Chilion and Mahlon. I have also acquired Ruth the Moabite, Mahlon's widow, as my wife, in order to maintain the name of the dead with his property, so that his name will not disappear from among his family or from his hometown. Today you are witnesses!"

Then the elders and all the people at the gate said, "We are witnesses. May the LORD make the woman who is coming into your home like Rachel and Leah, who together built up the family of Israel. May you have standing in Ephrathah and be famous in Bethlehem. Through the offspring the LORD gives you by this young woman, may your family be like that of Perez, whom Tamar bore to Judah."

—Ruth 4:7-12

What was the custom in Israel concerning the redemption and transfer of property?

_____

_____

What purpose did the custom serve? Do we have anything like this custom in our culture today?

_____

_____

What did the nameless guardian-redeemer of Naomi tell Boaz to do?

_____

_____

Why (according to Deuteronomy 25:7-9) was it fortunate for the guardian-redeemer that Boaz received the sandal and not Ruth?

_____

_____

According to the key passage, why did Boaz marry Ruth?

_____

_____

Who agreed to be the witnesses?

_____

_____

What blessing did the elders give to Ruth and Boaz?

_____

_____

How were Ruth and Boaz to be known in their city?

_____

_____

How were Ruth and Boaz to be like the "house of Perez"?

_____

_____

What is unusual about the birth of Perez in Genesis 38:24-30?

_____

_____

As you come to this portion of the story, what emotions do you feel for Boaz and Ruth?

_____

_____

We delight in mountaintop moments but we must guard ourselves from allowing our emotions to become overly involved. Though we rejoice in victory, we must also remember to rejoice through seasons of endurance.

Write Hebrews 13:8 below.

_____

_____

Whether you are on the mountain top or in a valley, God is unchanging. He is worthy of our thanksgiving and praise despite our circumstances. Take a moment to declare God's unwavering character in the midst of changing circumstances.

_____

_____

_____

_____

_____

_____

_____

_____

_____

_____

_____

_____

Week 5, Day 4

A New Life

Read Ruth 4

Key passage:

> *So Boaz took Ruth and she became his wife. When he made love to her, the LORD enabled her to conceive, and she gave birth to a son. The women said to Naomi: "Praise be to the LORD, who this day has not left you without a guardian-redeemer. May he become famous throughout Israel! He will renew your life and sustain you in your old age. For your daughter-in-law, who loves you and who is better to you than seven sons, has given him birth."*

> *Then Naomi took the child in her arms and cared for him. The women living there said, "Naomi has a son!" And they named him Obed. He was the father of Jesse, the father of David.*

> *This, then, is the family line of Perez:*

> *Perez was the father of Hezron, Hezron the father of Ram, Ram the father of Amminadab, Amminadab the father of Nahshon, Nahshon the father of Salmon, Salmon the father of Boaz, Boaz the father of Obed, Obed the father of Jesse, and Jesse the father of David.*

> —Ruth 4:13-22

Finally, Ruth and Boaz marry. When they have a son, how do the townswomen react? How do they bless Naomi?

_____

_____

How did the townswomen describe Ruth?

_____

What does this tell you about Ruth?

_____

_____

How did Naomi care for the young child?

_____

_____

Who would this new baby's grandson be?

_____

Which verses in Matthew 1 match Ruth 4:18-22?

_____

_____

Which verses in Luke 3 match Ruth 4:18-22?

_____

_____

What is the importance of the genealogy given in this passage?

_____

_____

In the first chapter of Ruth, we notice the townswomen ignoring Ruth's presence as she returns with Naomi to Bethlehem. Their opinion of Ruth has changed drastically from the beginning of the story.

When have you judged someone incorrectly and discovered they were far different/better than you first thought?

_____

_____

When have you misjudged unfairly?

_____

God not only redeemed Ruth's pain of loss by placing her with a faithful man, God redeemed Ruth's reputation.

What do you need God to redeem today? How do you hope God might redeem your pain or loss?

_____

_____

Write out a prayer and ask God to draw near as you walk the journey toward redemption. Ask Him for His strength to persevere and grace to walk through each day trusting Him with your story.

_____

_____

_____

_____

_____

_____

_____

_____

_____

Week 5, Day 5

Jesus, Our Kinsmen Redeemer

Read Ruth 4

Boaz was under no obligation to redeem Ruth, and yet he chose to do so, no matter what it cost him personally. For thousands of years, Christians have made the connection to the integrity seen in Boaz as a picture of Jesus and His love for us. He is our Redeemer, and He bought us with His blood.

A kinsman-redeemer must have four qualities in order to redeem: relation, willingness, ability, and the means (or price) to redeem the property or person.

Let's consider how Jesus meets these requirements for us.

Related:

What do the following verses say about Jesus' relation to humanity?

John 1:14_____

_____

Galatians 4:4_____

_____

Hebrews 2:14-15_____

_____

Willing:

What do the following verses say about Jesus' willingness to redeem us?

John 10:17-18_____

_____

Hebrews 12:2_____

_____

Able:

What do the following verses say about Jesus' ability to redeem us?

Romans 3:24_____

_____

Romans 5:8_____

_____

Hebrews 7:25_____

_____

Price:

What do the following verses say about the price Jesus paid to redeem us?

Romans 8:2-4_____

_____

Romans 3:23-24_____

_____

2 Corinthians 5:21_____

_____

Just as Boaz freely offered to be a kinsman-redeemer for Naomi and Ruth, Jesus freely offers to be your kinsman-redeemer.

Have you accepted Him as your kinsman-redeemer?

_____

How does Jesus as your redeemer change your story forever?

_____

_____

Just as you rejoiced for Ruth as she found redemption through Boaz, spend time rejoicing and thanking Jesus for the redemption you have found in Him.

_____

_____

_____

_____

_____

_____

_____

_____

_____

_____

_____

_____

6

with eyes wide open

notes:

notes:

Reflection

In what part of your story can you easily identify God moving and working in your life?

What parts of your story are harder to identify God at work?

Consider what parts of your story you can share that might honor God by recognizing Him at work!

REFERENCES

"Elimelech," Hitchcock's Bible Names Dictionary, accessed February 19, 2018, https://www.biblestudytools.com/dictionaries/hitchcocks-bible-names/elimelech.html

Gifford, Jerry, "The Burden and Bitterness of a Barren Life," accessed February 19, 2018, http://www.lifeway.com/Article/sermon-ruth-burden-bitterness-barenness-joy-fulfillment.

Holman Christian Standard Study Bible Notes, Nashville: Holman Bible Publishers. 2010

Hamilton, Pearl. Godly Living in Ungodly Times: Judges and Ruth. Honolulu: Discipler's Bible Study, 1991.

"Naomi," Smith's Bible Dictionary, accessed February 19, 2018, https://www.biblestudytools.com/dictionaries/smiths-bible-dictionary/naomi.html.

Rev. R. Sinker, "Ruth 1," Ellicott's Commentary for English Readers, accessed February 19, 2018, http://biblehub.com/commentaries/ellicott/ruth/1.htm.

Gifford, Jerry, "The Burden and Bitterness of a Barren Life," accessed February 19, 2018, http://www.lifeway.com/Article/sermon-ruth-burden-bitterness-barenness-joy-fulfillment.

ABOUT THE AUTHOR

Bobi Ann Allen is a pastor's wife, mom, and ministry leader. She was raised in a small East Texas town and now calls Central Texas home. A graduate of Liberty Baptist Theological Seminary with a master's degree in Christian education, Bobi Ann's greatest passion in ministry is to open the Word with women and let the Holy Spirit transform hearts—including her own. She spends her days folding underwear, unloading the dishwasher, and hunting for her people's lost stuff. Bobi Ann loves to laugh, spend time with her husband, Jared, and her delightfully silly kids, Kati Ann and Kie. You can find more from Bobi Ann on her website bobiann.com and by following her on Facebook and Instagram @bobiann.

50103325R00067

Made in the USA
Columbia, SC
02 February 2019